ANIMALS
A PICTURE SOURCEBOOK
EDITED AND ARRANGED BY DON RICE

Over 700 copyright-free illustrations for direct copying and reference.

VNR VAN NOSTRAND REINHOLD COMPANY
New York Cincinnati Toronto London Melbourne

Published in 1979 by Van Nostrand Reinhold Company
A division of Litton Educational Publishing, Inc.
135 West 50th Street, New York, NY 10020, U.S.A.

Van Nostrand Reinhold Limited
1410 Birchmount Road
Scarborough, Ontario M1P 2E7, Canada

Van Nostrand Reinhold Australia Pty. Ltd.
17 Queen Street
Mitcham, Victoria 3132, Australia

Van Nostrand Reinhold Company Limited
Molly Millars Lane
Wokingham, Berkshire, England

16 15 14 13 12 11 10 9 8 7 6 5 4 3

Library of Congress Cataloging in Publication Data

Main entry under title:

Animals, a picture sourcebook.

 Includes index.
 1. Animals in art. 2. Illustration of books.
I. Rice, Donald L.
NC961.7.A54A54 760 79-12871
ISBN 0-442-26102-0

Introduction

The illustrations in this bestiary were drawn or engraved over a period of 100 years, from the early 1800s to the early 1900s, by innumerable artists with a wide variety of skills, styles, and knowledge about their subjects. Many are beautifully executed and very accurate. Some, such as the ferocious dolphins and smiling orangutan, are quite fanciful. All have useful applications for artists, students, and researchers. The collection is intended to serve as three books in one:

Clip Book

Up to 10 illustrations may be copied directly for each graphic arts project without obtaining further permission from the publisher. A credit line, though not necessary, would be appreciated.

Source Book

As a portable artist's "swipe file" it will provide a handy guide in the creation of original drawings and paintings of animals.

Reference Book

The animals pictured are alphabetically categorized first by order (indicated by a solid black line), then by family (broken line), and then species (with occasional lapses in alphabetizing to accommodate page layouts). It seemed unnecessary for the purposes of this book to divide the families into genera. Similarly suborders, superfamilies, and the like have been disregarded with one exception: the division of the order *Cetacea* into the suborders *Mystacoceti* and *Odontoceti*.

Mammals were not systematically classified to any reasonable degree until Linnaeus published the 10th edition of his *Systema Naturae* in 1785. Since that time there have been radical changes in the approaches to scientific classification. Revisions are still being made. It is highly probable that some readers will disagree with the inclusion of certain species within certain families, e.g., the giant panda has been at times classified as both a member of the *Ursidae* family (bears) and the *Procyonidae* (raccoons). In this book it is included with the bears. There are other possible areas of disagreement. Seals and walruses, for example, have been considered as both a suborder under *Carnivora* and as a separate order unto themselves. I have treated them as an order (*Pinnipedia*).

Readers may also find some out-and-out mistakes. They are encouraged to bring these to my attention by writing to the publisher.

Don Rice

Contents

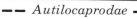

Pronghorn

Pronghorn

Pronghorn

Pronghorn

Bovidae

Addax

Aurochs

Aoudad

Argali, Thibet

Bighorn Sheep

Bison

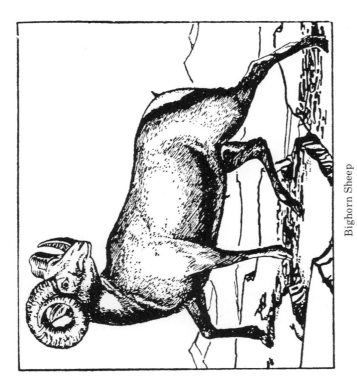

Bighorn Sheep

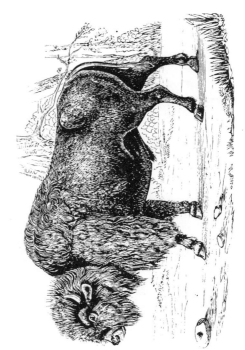

Bison

Bison

Bison

Bison

Blackbuck

Blesbok

Bluebuck

Bubale

Bushbuck

Cambing-utan

Cape Buffalo

Chamois

Chamois

Chamois

Chamois

Eland

Duykerbok

Eland

Forest Ox

Cows and Calf

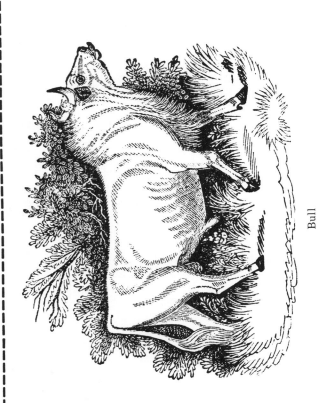

Bull

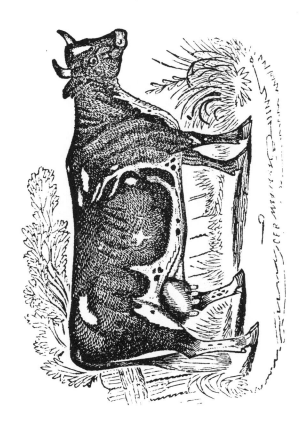

Cow

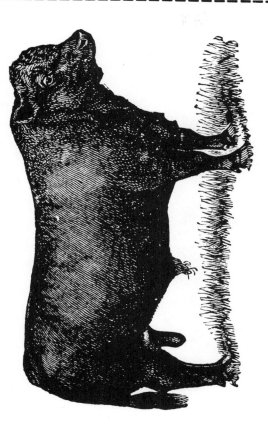

Aberdeen Angus

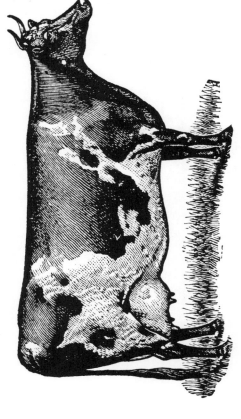

Ayershire

Cow of Bazadois

Cow of Bearn

Breton Bull

Charolaise Bull

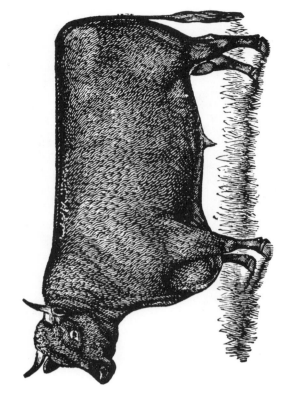

Devon Bull

Durham Polled Cow

Dutch Belted Bull

Galloway Bull

Bull of La Garonne

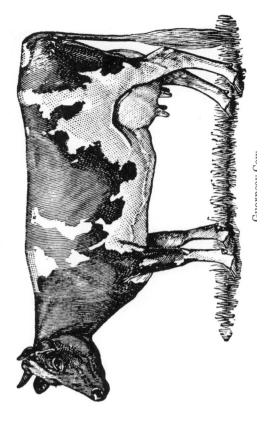

Guernsey Cow

Hereford Steer

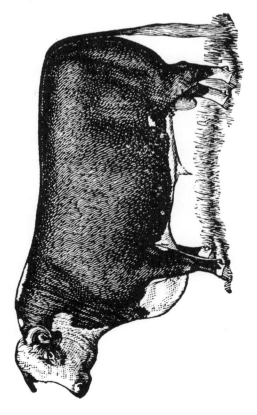

Hereford Bull

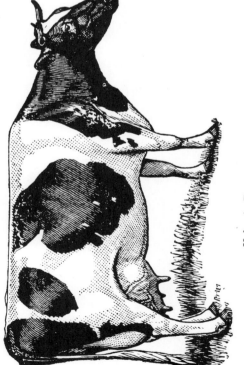

Holstein-Friesian Cow

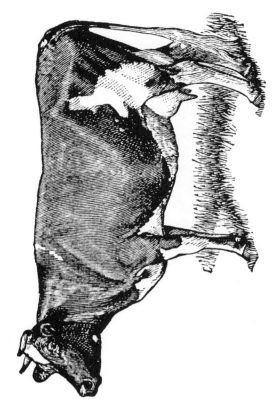

Jersey Cow

Norman Bull

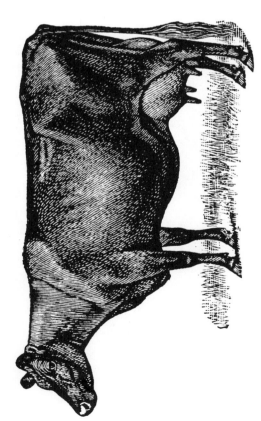

Red Polled Cow

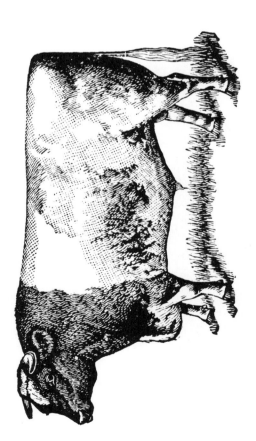

Shorthorn Bull

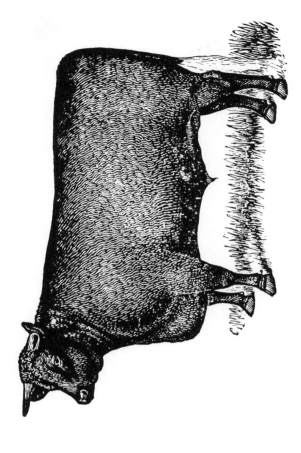

Sussex Steer

Swiss Cow

Texas Longhorn Steer

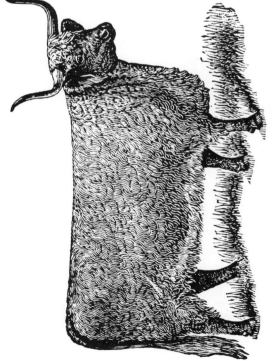

West Highland Cow

11

Four-horned Antelope

Gaur

Gazelle

Gazelle

Gnu

Brindled Gnu

Gnu

Gnu

Gnu

Hartebeest

Ibex

Ibex

Goat

Goat

Angora Goat

Angora Goat

Cashmere Goat

Cashmere Goat

Kebsch

Klipspringer

Kudu

Kudu

Kudu

Madoqua

Muntjac

Mouflon

Musk Ox

Musk Ox

Nilgai

Nilgai

Nilgai

Gemsbok

Ourebi

Oryx, Abyssinian

Draught Oxen

Hungarian Oxen

Reebok

Persian Wild Goat

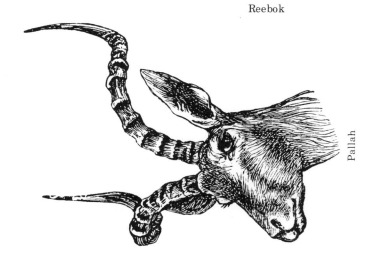

Pallah

Rocky Mountain Goat

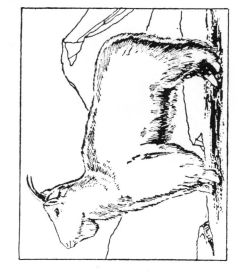

Rocky Mountain Goat

Rocky Mountain Goat

Rocky Mountain Goat

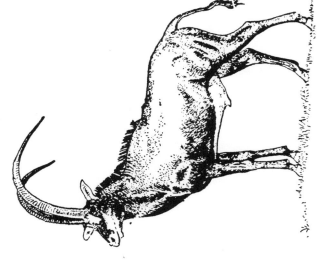

Sable Antelope

Sable Antelope

Sable Antelope

Saiga

Sakeen

Sassaby

Saiga

Sheep

Sheep

Black Breed of the Landes (Ram)

Blackfaced Highland Ram

Cheviot Ewe

Cotswold Ewe

Cotswold Ram

Cotswold Ewe

Dorset Horn Ram

Fat-tailed

Hampshire Down Ram

Breed of Larzac

Leicester

Leicester Ewe

Lincoln Ram

Lincoln Ram

Delaine Merino Ram

American Merino Ram

Merino Ram

Mauchamp Merino Ram

Rambouillet Merino Ram and Ewe

Merino Ram

Shropshire

Oxfordshire Down

Rambouillet

Shropshire

Southdown

Southdown

Touareg Ram

Welsh Ram

Singsing

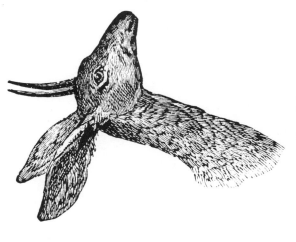

Springbok

Springbok

Springbok

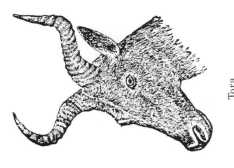

Tora

Steenbok

Urial

Wariatu

Water-buck

Water Buffalo

Zebu

Water Buffalo

Zebu

Zebu

Yak

Alpaca

Bactrian Camel

Arabian Camel

Alpaca

Bactrian Camel

Arabian Camel

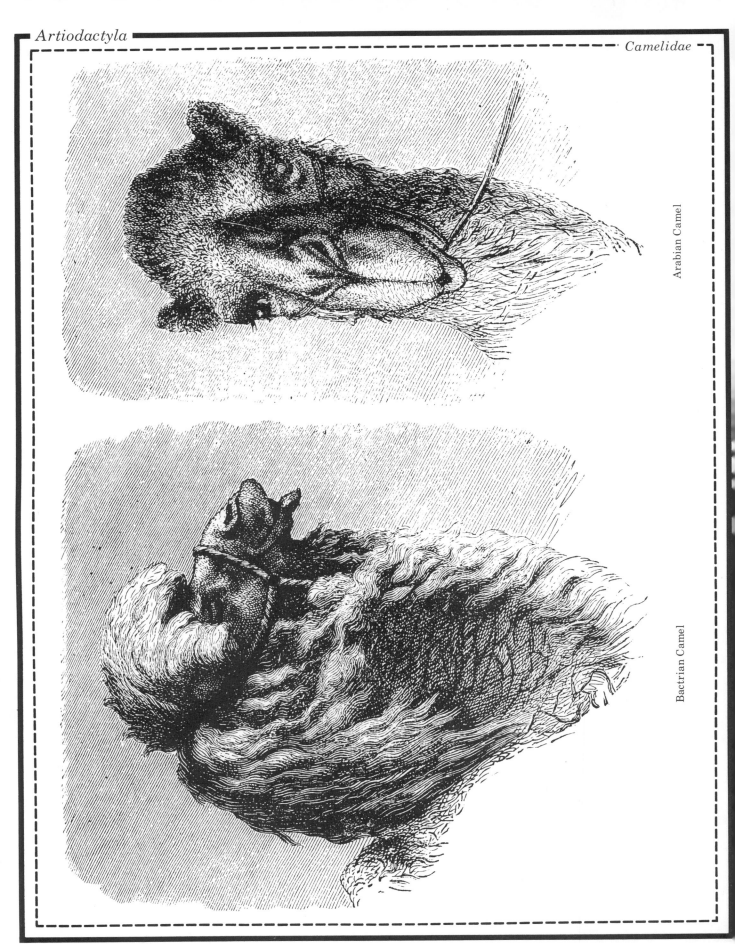

Arabian Camel

Bactrian Camel

Arabian Camel

Arabian Camel

Guanaco

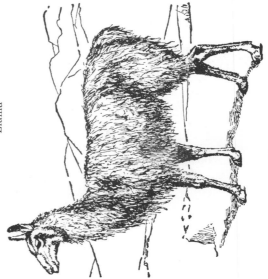

Llama

Llama

Camelidae

Cervidae

Axis Hind

Vicuna

Axis

Woodland Caribou

Barren-ground Caribou

Caribou

European Elk

Fallow Deer

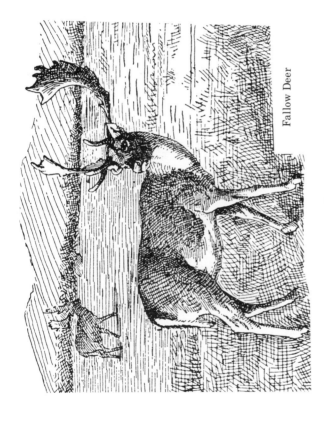

Fallow Deer

Fallow Deer

Moose

Moose

Moose

Moose

Moose

Moose

Moose

Mule Deer

Mule Deer

Musk Deer

Père David's Deer

Pigmy Musk Deer

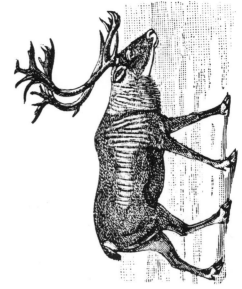

Reindeer

Reindeer

Reindeer

Reindeer

Reindeer

Reindeer

Reindeer

Reindeer

Roebuck

Sika

Roe Deer

Roebuck

Virginia Deer

Virginia Deer

Sambar

Wapiti

Wapiti

Wapiti

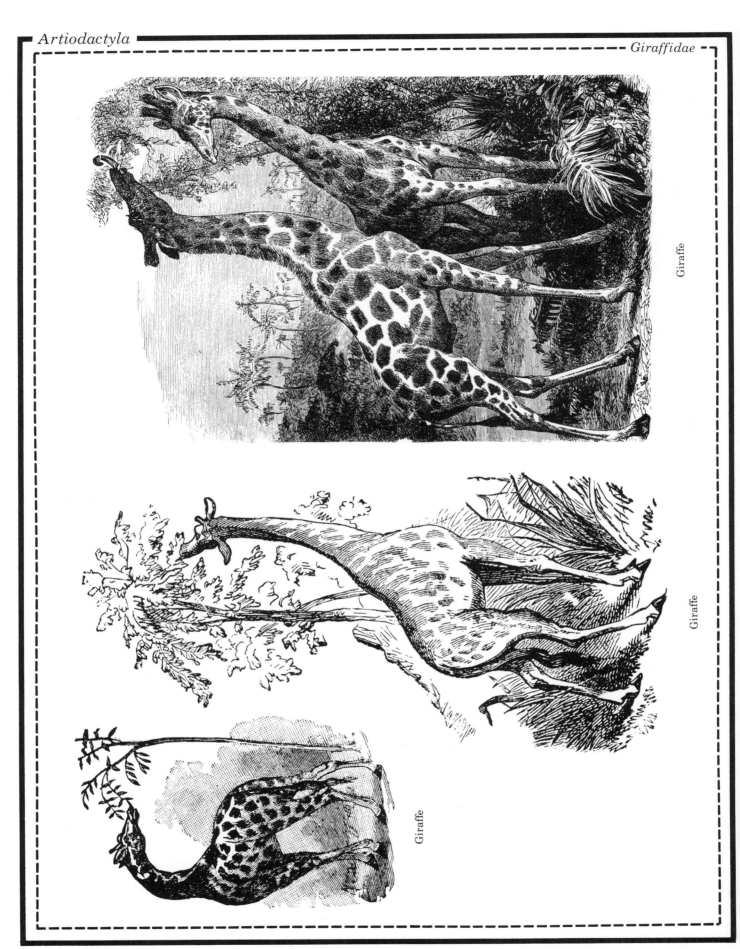

Giraffe

Giraffe

Giraffe

Giraffe

Giraffe

Giraffe

Okapi

Hippopotamus

Hippopotamus

Hippopotamus

Babiroussa

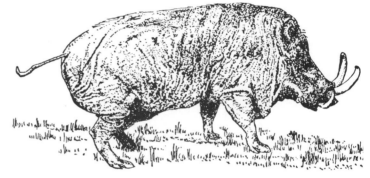

Babiroussa

Boschvark

Wart Hog

Wart Hog

Wild Boar

Wild Boar

Berkshire Boar

Berkshire Boar

Bressane Sow

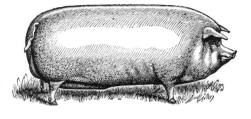

Chester White Boar

Duroc-Jersey Boar

Craonnese Boar

English White Boar

Wild Boar

Pigs

Essex Sow

Perigord Boar

Poland-China Boar

Tamworth Boar

Yorkshire Boar

Tayassuidae

White-lipped Peccary

Collared Peccary

African Hunting Dog

Coyote

Coyote

Coyote

Dingo Dhole

Fennec

Fox

Silver Fox

Silver Fox

Fox

Fox

Fox

Jackal

Jackal

Pied Thous

Wolf

Wolf

Wolf

Wolf

African Bloodhound

Airedale

Basset

Beagle

Bloodhound

Bedlington Terrier

Boston Terrier

Bulldogs

Bulldog

Bulldog

Bull Terrier

Bull Terrier

Bull Terrier

Cocker Spaniel

Collie

Collie

Dachshound

Collie

Dandie Dinmont

Dachshound

Deerhound

English Setter

Eskimo Dog

English Setter

Eskimo Dog

Eskimo Dog

Foxhound

Foxhound

Smooth Fox Terrier

Smooth Fox Terrier

Wire-haired Fox Terrier

Gascony Hound

French Black Poodle

Great Dane

Great Dane

Great Dane

Greyhound

Greyhound

Havanese

Highland Hound

Japanese Spaniel

Irish Water Spaniel

Land Spaniel

Large French Water Spaniel

Mastiff

Mastiff

Newfoundland

Newfoundland

Newfoundland

Newfoundland

Pointer

Pointer

Pointer

Pointer

Poodle

Pug

Pyrenean Shepherd

Russian Wolfhound

Saint Bernard, Rough-coated

Saint Bernard, Rough-coated

Saint Bernard, Smooth-coated

Scotch Terrier

Scotch Terrier

Scotch Terrier

Schipperke

Setter

Skye Terrier

Turnspit

Warwickshire Foxhound

Yorkshire Terrier

Angora

Bobcat

Caracal

Cheeta

Chaus

Cheeta

Cougar

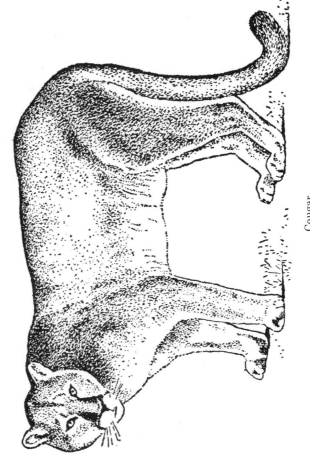

Cougar

Domestic Cat

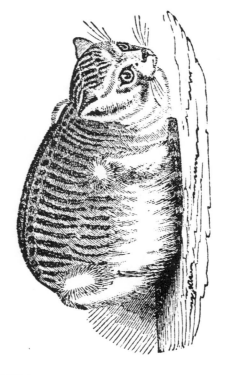

Domestic Cat

Eyra

Jaguar

Jaguar

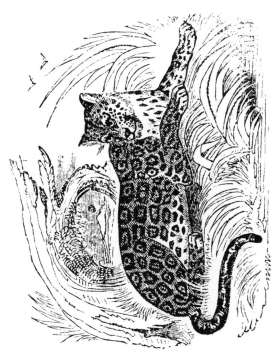

Jaguar

Jaguarundi

Leopard

Leopard

Leopard

Leopard

Leopard

European Lynx

Canadian Lynx

Canadian Lynx

Lion

Lion

Lion

Lion

Persian Lion

Lion

Lion

Ocelot

Serval

Ocelot

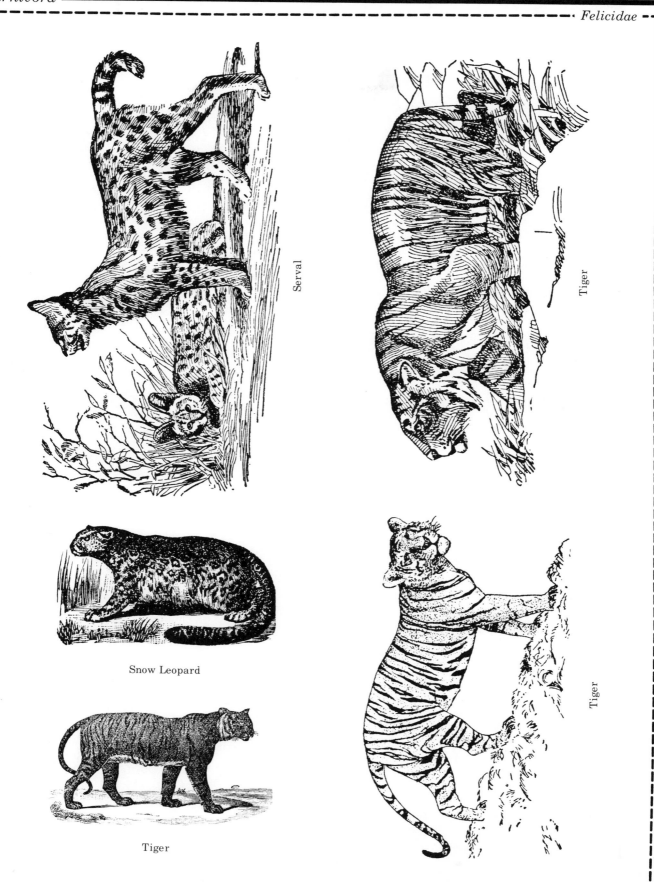

Serval

Tiger

Snow Leopard

Tiger

Tiger

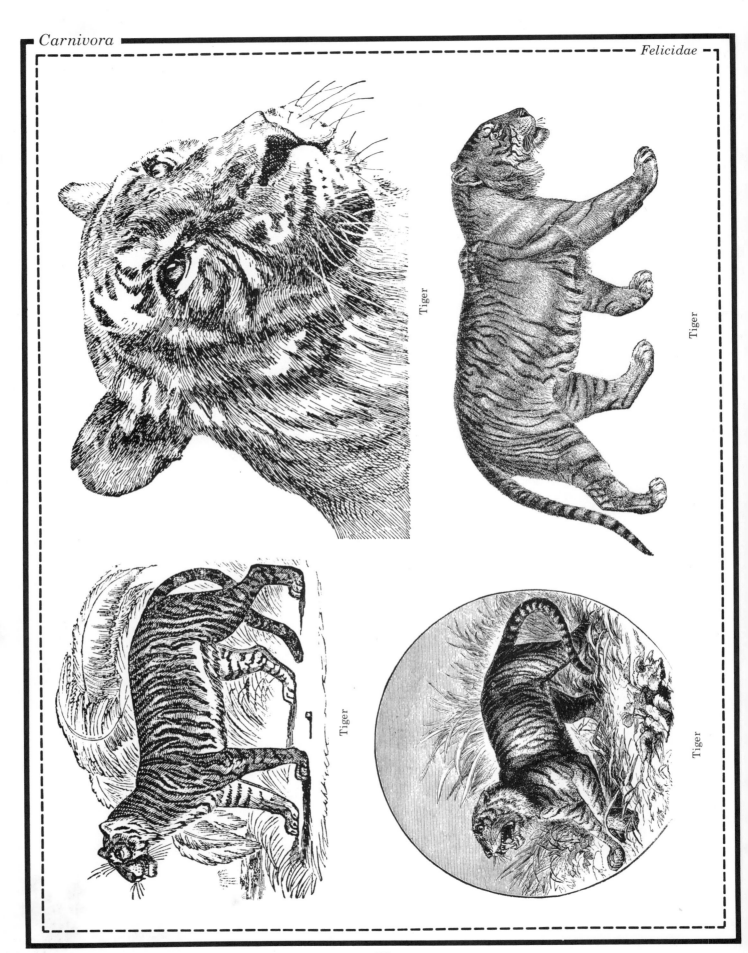

Tiger

Tiger

Tiger

Tiger

Tiger

European Wild Cat

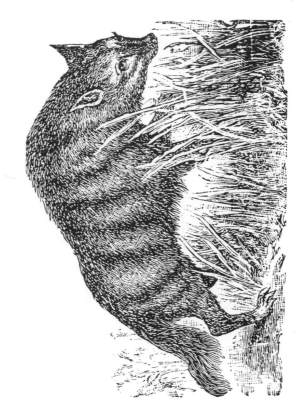

Aardwolf

Aardwolf

Hyena

Spotted Hyena

Badger

Common Badger

American Badger

Balisaur

Ferret

Ferret

Beech Marten

Fisher

Otter

Pine Marten

Polecat

European Otter

Polecat

European Polecat

Otter

Ratel

Ratel

Sea Otter

Skunk

Skunk

Skunk

Skunk

Winter Coat

Summer Coat

Least Weasel

Summer Coat

Winter Coat

Shorttail Weasel

Longtail Weasel

Shorttail Weasel

Wolverine

Wolverine

Wolverine

African Zorii

Procyonidae

Kinkajou

Coati-mondi

Raccoon

Coati-mondi

Raccoon

Raccoon

Raccoon

Black Bear

Black Bear

Brown Bear

Black Bear

Brown Bear

Grizzly Bear

Brown Bear

Grizzly Bear

Grizzly Bear

Grizzly Bear

Kodiak Bear

Malay Bear

Malay Bear

Sloth Bear

Giant Panda

Giant Panda

Spectacled Bear

Polar Bear

Polar Bear

Polar Bear

Polar Bear

Cacomistle

Binturong

Civet

Civet

Civet

Genet

Palm Civit

Mongoose

Suricate

Urva

Right Whale

Right Whale

Cetacea (Sub-order *Mystacoceti*)

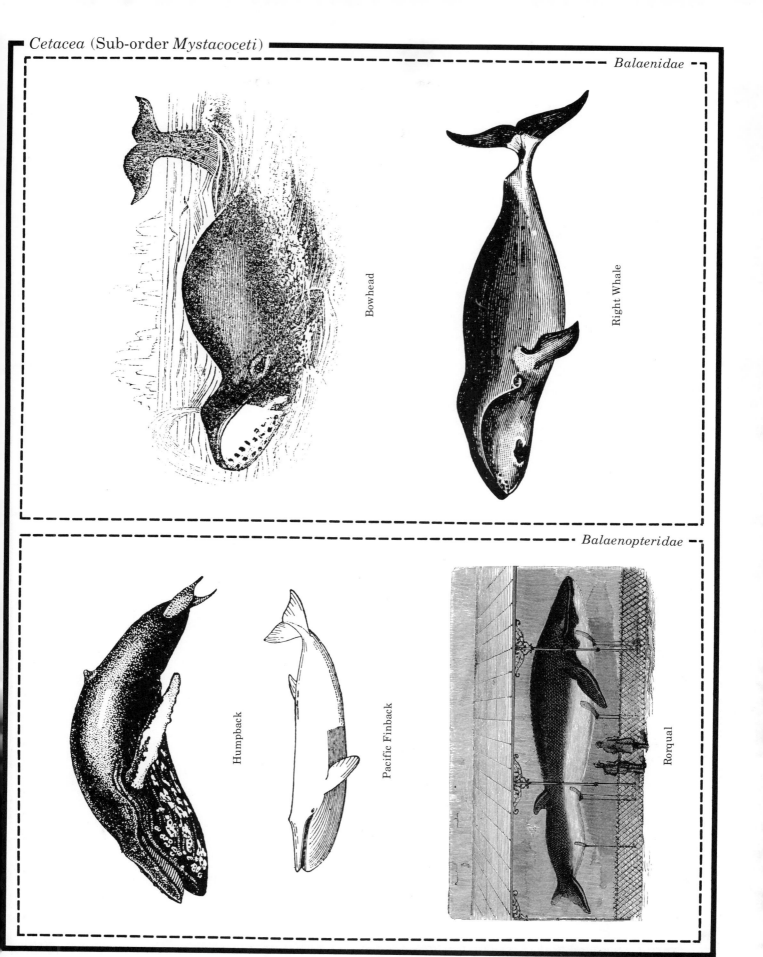

Balaenidae

Bowhead

Right Whale

Balaenopteridae

Humpback

Pacific Finback

Rorqual

Dolphin

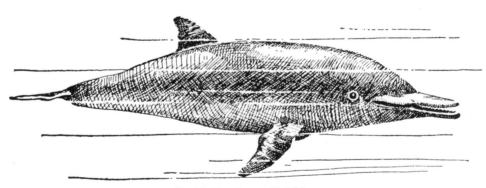

Pacific Bottlenose Dolphin

Narwhale

Narwhale

Narwhale

Atlantic Harbor Porpoise

Porpoise

Dall Porpoise

Sperm Whale

Cetacea (Sub-order *Odontoceti*)

Physeridae

Sperm Whale

Ziphiidae

Bottlenose Whale

Chiroptera

Desmodontidae

Spectre Vampire

Javelin Vampire

Spectre Vampire

Megadermatidae

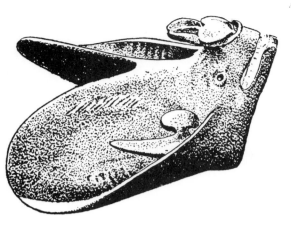

Big-eared Bat

Phyllostomatidae

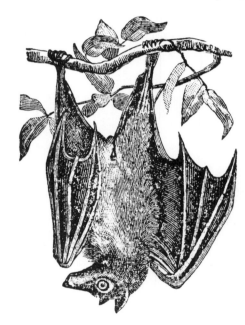

Leaf-nosed Bat

Pteropidae

Flying Fox

Flying Fox

Kalong

Vespertilionidae

Long-eared Bat

Vespertilionidae

Long-eared Bat

Hoary Bat

Pipistrelle

Edentata

Bradypodidae

Two-toed Sloth

Three-toed Sloth

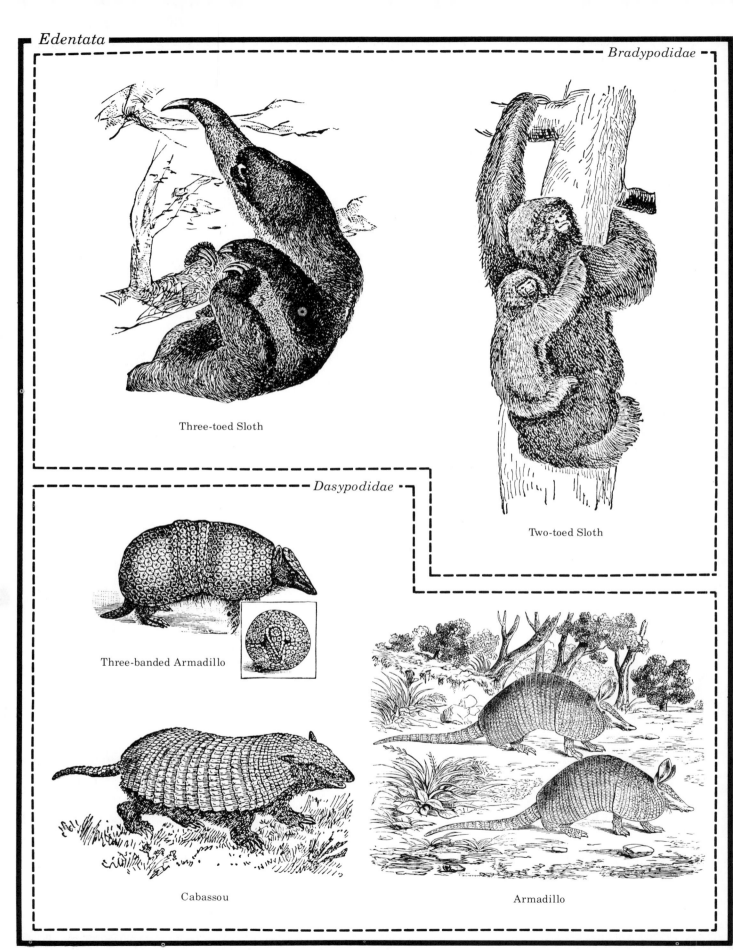

Bradypodidae

Dasypodidae

Three-toed Sloth

Two-toed Sloth

Three-banded Armadillo

Cabassou

Armadillo

Giant Anteater

Giant Anteater

Giant Anteater

Giant Anteater

Australian Anteater

Tamandua

Procaviidae

Erinacidae

Daman

Gymnure

Soricidae

Desman

Hedgehog

Pyrenean Desman

Common Shrew

Common Shrew

Common Shrew

Elephant Shrew

Elephant Shrew

Tree Shrew

Water Shrew

Indian Sondeli

Rat-tailed Sondeli

Insectivora

Talpidae

Mole

Mole

Tenracidae

Tenrec

Tupaidae

Banxring

Lagomorpha

Leporidae

Lagotis

Hare

Tame Rabbit

Wild Rabbit

Rabbit

Wild Rabbit

Leporidae

Rabbit

Rabbit

Rabbit

Rabbit

Marsupialia

Dasyuridae

Spotted Dasyure

Tasmanian Devil

Tasmanian Wolf

Tasmanian Wolf

Australian Opossum

Opossum

Murine Opossum

Didelphidae

Macropodidae

Filander

Virginia Opossum

Tufted-tailed Rat-kangaroo

Giant Kangaroo

Giant Kangaroo

Macropodidae

Phalangeridae

Spotted Cuscus

Giant Kangaroo

Phalanger

Sooty Phalanger

Vulpine Phalanger

Phascolomidae

Koala

Koala

Wombat

Wombat

Monotremata

Orithorhynchidae

Duck-billed Platypus

Duck-billed Platypus

Monotremata

Orithorhynchidae

Tachyglossidae

Duck-billed Platypus

Echidna

Perissodactyla

Equidae

Domestic Ass

Domestic Ass

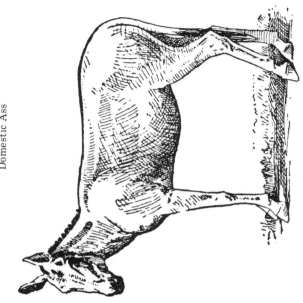

Wild Ass

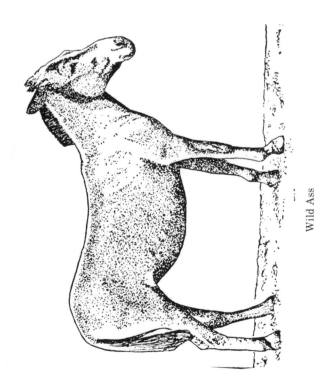

Wild Ass

Domestic Ass

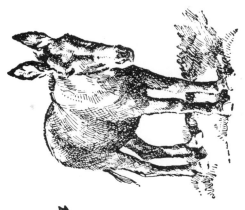

Burro

Kiang

Kiang

Kiang

Mule

Mule

Przewalski's Horse

Quagga

Burchell's Zebra

Zebra

Zebra

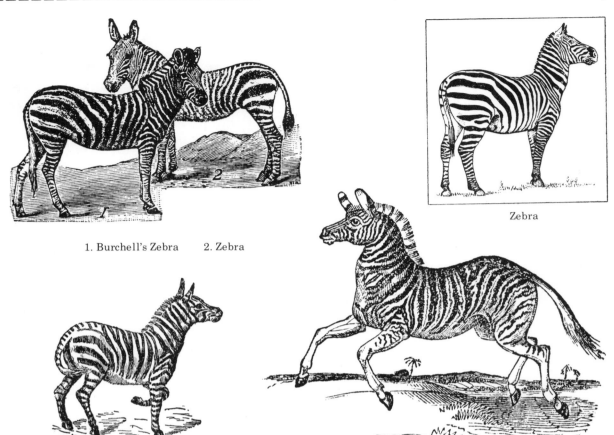

1. Burchell's Zebra 2. Zebra

Zebra

Zebra

Zebra

Arabian Horse

Arabian Horse

Belgian

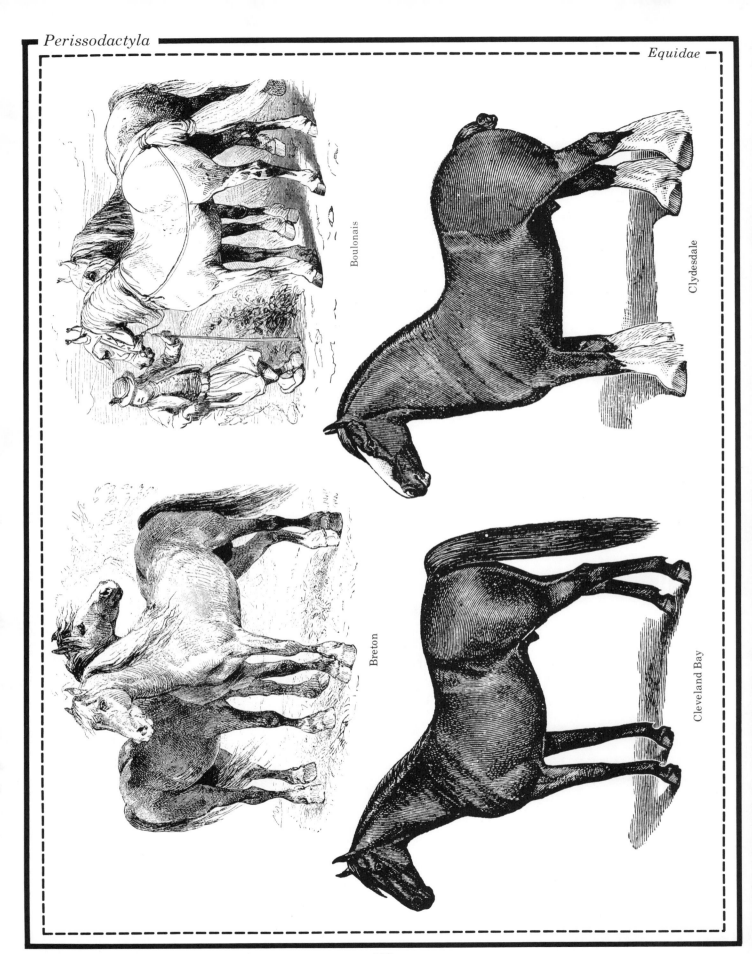

Boulonais

Clydesdale

Breton

Cleveland Bay

Draft Horse

English Race Horse

German Coach Horse

German Coach Horse

French Coach Horse

Indian Pony

Orloff

Hackney

Pacer

Norman

Percheron

Percheron

Pyrenean

Russian

Shetland Pony

Shetland Pony

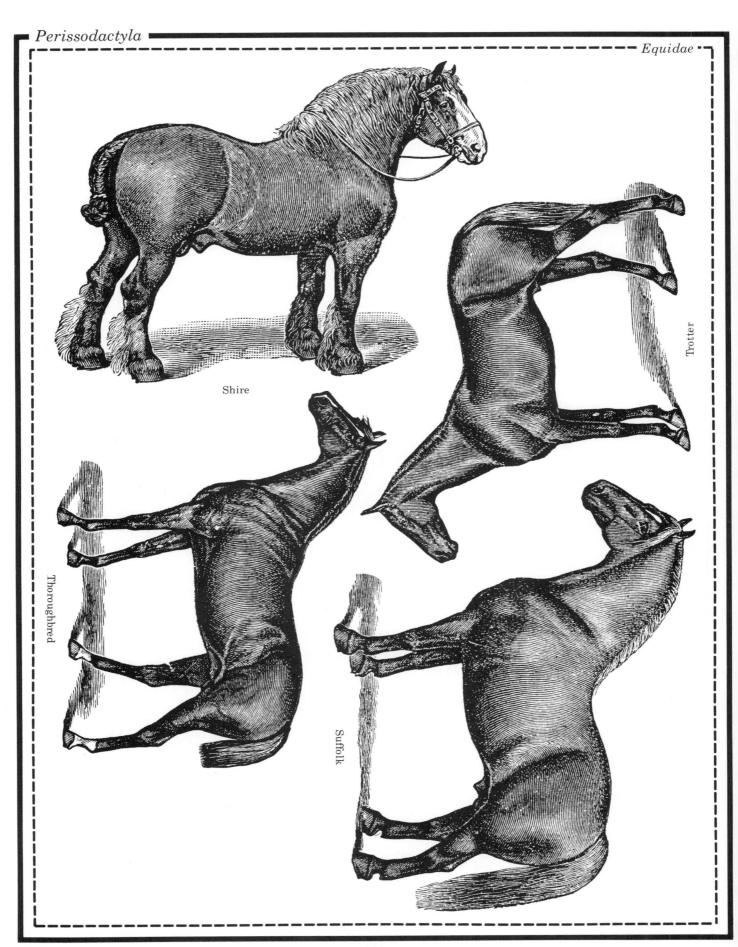

Shire

Trotter

Thoroughbred

Suffolk

Indian Rhinoceros

African Rhinoceros

Indian Rhinoceros

Indian Rhinoceros

Indian Rhinoceros

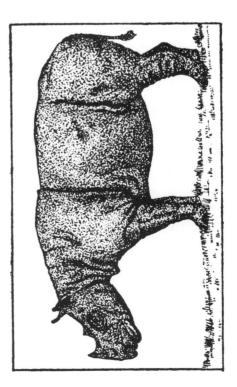

Indian Rhinoceros

African Rhinoceros

South American Tapir

South American Tapir Malayan Tapir

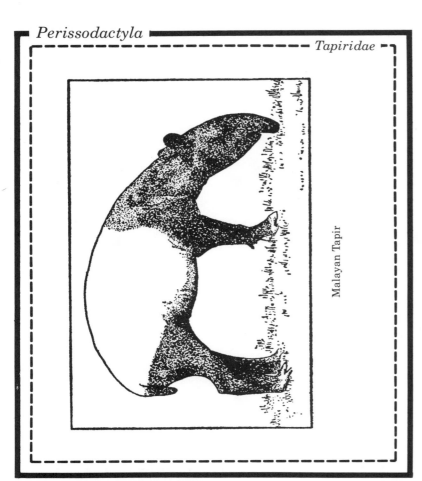

Malayan Tapir

Short-tailed Pangolin

Walrus

Walrus

Walrus

Otariidae

Fur Seal

Crested Seal

Fur Seal

Sea Lion

Stellar Sea Lion

Elephant Seal

Harbor Seal

Marmoset

Marmoset

Bearded Saki

Capuchin

Capuchin

Collared Squirrel Monkey

Douroucouli

Monkey

Ouakari

Sapajou

Ursine Howler

Ursine Howler

Spider Monkey

Baboon

Bonnet Macaque

Gelada

Barbary Ape

Chacma Baboon

Grivet

Guinea Baboon

Guereza

Lion-tailed Macaque

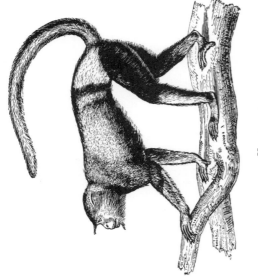

Hanuman

Mandrill

Mandrill

Rhesus

Colobidae

White-nosed Monkey

Proboscis

Colobidae

Proboscis

Langur

Daubentoniidae

Aye-Aye

Aye-Aye

Lemuroidae

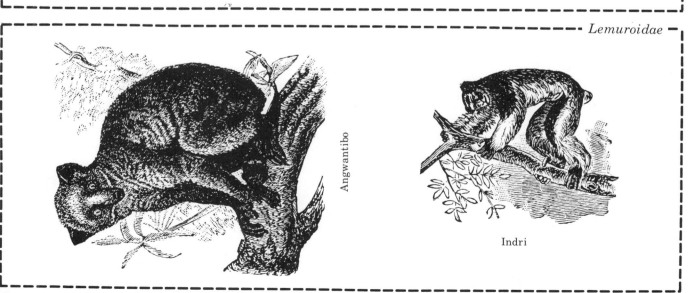

Angwantibo

Indri

129

Colugo

Handed Lemur

Ring-tailed Lemur

White-footed Lemur

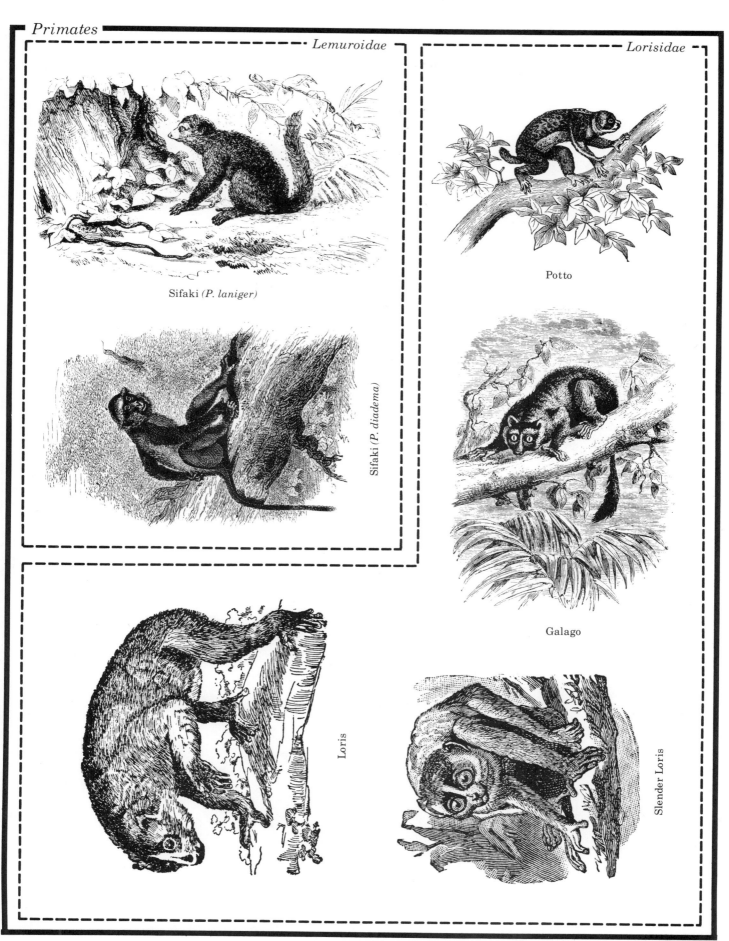

Lemuroidae

Lorisidae

Sifaki *(P. laniger)*

Sifaki *(P. diadema)*

Potto

Galago

Loris

Slender Loris

Chimpanzee

Chimpanzee

Gorilla

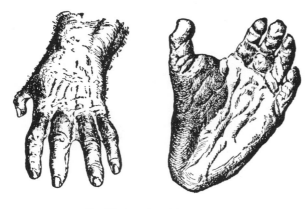

Gorilla hand and foot

Gorilla

Hoolock

Orangutan

Orangutan

Orangutan

Orangutan

Unga-puti

Siaming

White-handed Gibbon

Tarsier

Tarsier

Probiscidea

Elephantidae

African Elephant

African Elephant

African Elephant

Indian Elephant

Indian Elephant

Indian Elephant

Indian Elephant

Indian Elephant

Indian Elephant

Indian Elephant

Indian Elephant

Indian Elephant

Indian Elephant

Indian Elephant

Indian Elephant

Rodentia

Anomaluridae

African Flying Squirrel

Capromydae

Coypou

Castoridae

Beaver

Beaver

Beaver

Beaver

Beaver

Beaver

Beaver

Capybara

Capybara

Guinea Pig

Guinea Pig

Capybara

Guinea Pig

Guinea Pig

Chinchilla

Chinchilla

Viscacha

Viscacha

European Field Vole

Hamster

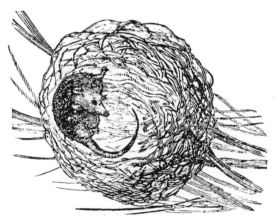

Harvest Mouse

Harvest Mouse

Harvest Mouse

Florida Wood Rat

Hudson's Bay Lemming

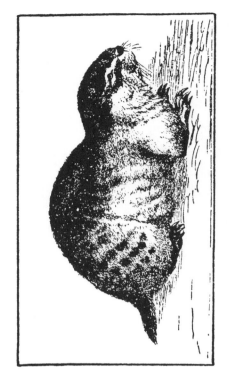

European Lemming

Meadow Mouse

Lemming

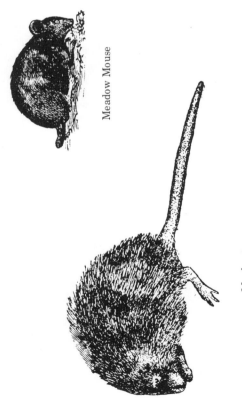

Muskrat

Muskrat

Ctyenomyidae

Tuco-tuco

Cuniculidae

Sooty Paca

Dasyproctidae

Agouti

Agouti

Agouti

Agouti

Jerboa

Jerboa

Jerboa

Erethizonidae

Geomyidae

N. American Porcupine

N. American Porcupine

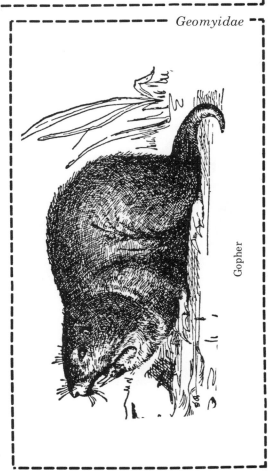

Gopher

Geomyidae

Plains Pocket Gopher

Northern Pocket Gopher

Gliridae

Dormouse

Dormouse

Heteromyidae

Kangaroo Rat

Hystricidae

Bush-tailed Porcupine

European Porcupine

European Porcupine

European Porcupine

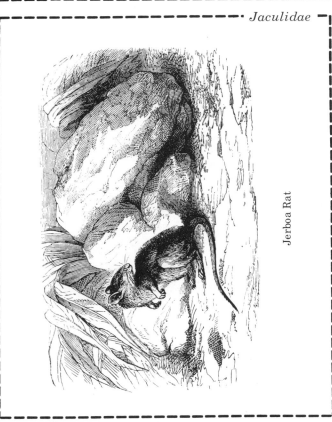

Jerboa Rat

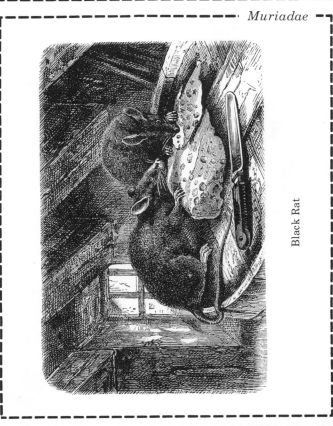

Black Rat

Short-tailed Field Mouse

House Mouse

House Mouse

Norway Rat

Norway Rat

Muriadae

Water Rat

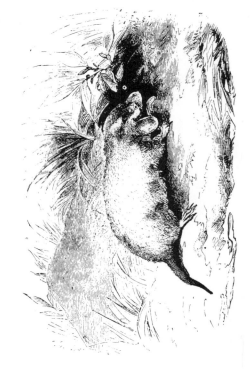

Pouched Rat

Norway Rat

Water Rat

Ochotonidae

Pika

Peramelidae

Rabbit Bandicoot

Chipmunk

American Flying Squirrel

European Squirrel

Gray Squirrel

European Squirrel

European Squirrel

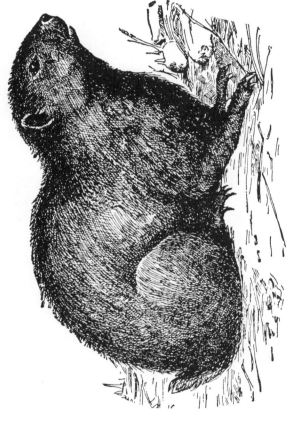

Groundhog

Groundhog

Prairie Dog

Marmot

Sciuridae

Red Squirrel

Siffleur

Pigmy Petaurist

Thirteen-lined Ground Squirrel

Thirteen-lined Ground Squirrel

Thrynomydae

Spalacidae

Ground Pig

Mole Rat

Rodentia

Zapodidae

Jumping Mouse

Sirenia

Dugongidae

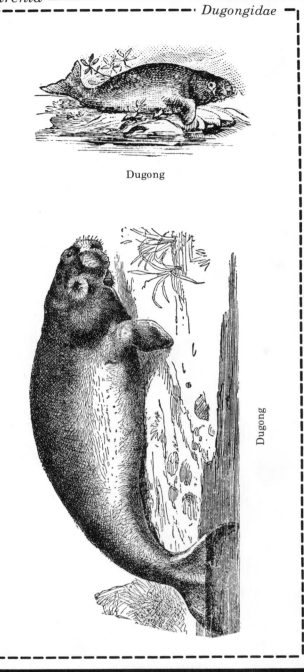

Dugong

Dugong

Trichechidae

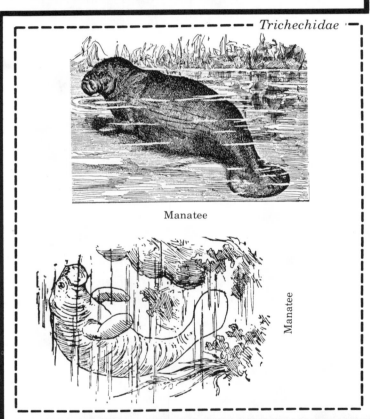

Manatee

Manatee

Tubulidentata

Orycteropodidae

Aardvark

Aardvark

Index